Janah Juma Obaid Salim Almarashda is a student in the GEMS Winchester Fujairah school. She is 11 years old and she has several hobbies, such as reading stories in the English language and making friends, as she is social.

Janah Juma Almarashda

My Poem

AUSTIN MACAULEY PUBLISHERS®
LONDON • CAMBRIDGE • NEW YORK • SHARJAH

ISBN – 9789948747192 – (Paperback)
ISBN – 9789948747208 – (E-Book)

Application Number: MC-10-01-3786014
Age Classification: 6-9

The age group that matches the content of the books has been classified according to the age classification system issued by the UAE Media Council.

First Published 2024
AUSTIN MACAULEY PUBLISHERS FZE
Sharjah Publishing City
P.O Box [519201]
Sharjah, UAE
www.austinmacauley.ae
+971 655 95 202

To my family.

My mother, Hind, my father, Juma, my two brothers, Hassan and Hamdan. I thank you for your support and encouragement of my writing.

The Numbers

One... it's time for fun,
Two... we have some things to do,
Three... I sat on a tree,
Four... someone has a loud snore,
Five... time to go for a dive,
Six... done now, I have to pick up bricks,
Seven... no silly, we don't have number eleven,
Eight... I really hate it when they close the gate,
Nine... I love it when the sun shines,
Ten... I have to borrow a pen.

5
6
7
4
8
2
9
1
3
10

The Garden

I can see a beautiful tree
Standing right next to me,
The smell of the lovely flowers
When suddenly my body overpowers,
I had the time of my life
I imagined that one flower had eyes,
But I had to go home
I had a package with Styrofoam.

The Jungle

I was in the jungle long ago
Where I had soggy, wet clothes,
I was smelling some flowers
When my body overpowers,
So I ate some delicious fruits
And then came down a lovely newt,
Oh look, a beautiful waterfall
Ahh! There's a dragon breathing fire balls,
Phew! We're finally okay
Oh, let's rest in that gray rock over there.

The Fruits

Apple is a basic
People eat it when they lay sick,
Orange has a lot of Vitamin C
People eat it so they break free,
Bananas are so yummy
It's healthier than a gummy,
Lemons are so sour
It feels like I have a super power,
Kiwi... kiwi... kiwi
We have to eat it sweetly.

The Weather

Maybe it will be sunny
So I could enjoy my honey,
Or maybe cloudy
So I could sing loudly,
Or rainy
So you cannot blame me,
Or a TORNADO
I better go hide my play dough,
A HURRICANE!
I must cancel the flight in the plane.

The Animals

Let's start off with a dog
But he was on a log,
Oh look! A cat
His name is Matt,
A horse
He loves to play sports,
A cow
No, it does not meow,
A cute hamster
Oh, he's running faster.

By Janah

The End